A

PICTURE HISTORY

OF THE

GRENVILLE FAMILY

OF

ROSEDALE HOUSE

A

PICTURE  HISTORY

of the

XXXXXXX GRENVILLE FAMILY XXXXXXX

of

ROSEDALE HOUSE

by Mary Yelloly, eight and a half years old

Preface by Helena Bonham Carter
Foreword by Simon Finch
Text by Lindsay Stainton

First published in the United States of America in 2007
by Rizzoli International Publications, Inc.
300 Park Avenue South
New York, NY 10010
www.rizzoliusa.com

2007 2008 2009/ 10 9 8 7 6 5 4 3 2 1

Designed by Minnie Weisz

Printed in Italy

ISBN: 0-8478-2922-7
ISBN 13: 978-0-8478-2922-4

Library of Congress Control Number: 2006934770

∞ Contents ∞

Preface

You hold in your hand a picture of a short life, a pocketful of delight, and maybe even a tiny time machine. Mary Yelloly lived just after Jane Austen wrote, and although her name sounds deliciously fictional, her life was real, as was her death from consumption at the age of 21. But though she barely made it into adulthood, she and her family will live forever through the world she created in this book. At the age of 8½, with her mother's encouragement, she began painting the first of what would become a four-volume work, a semi-fictional illustrated story of an imaginary family called the Grenvilles. If you lived then, you would have called it a pictorial history; today, it could be described as a surrogate photo album, a cartoon, a two-dimensional dollhouse, or a documentary of a certain type of 19th-century middle class country life. And because it is by a child, it is delightfully unvarnished, a through-the-keyhole glimpse into another time, a child's wave from 200 years ago.

Somebody clever wrote that although a woman may get older, it doesn't mean that she loses all the ages that she once was. I remember when I was young, I could look at pictures and jump right into them, like Mary Poppins and the children jumping into Bert's drawing on the pavement. Even though I'm now 40½, when I look at Mary's pictures, I remember that I'm also 8½, and I'm able to jump right back into them. So welcome, my fellow armchair time-travelers. Let Mary take you by the hand and have a stroll into her world. Go, you might get lost – and go on holiday for a few magical, enchanting Yelloly moments.

Helena Bonham Carter

Foreword

'Bibliomania' is a well-documented disease in which the victim endlessly pursues the un-findable. As a bookseller, I seek the extraordinary, the un-findable, rather than the blockbuster of weighty import. It is, of course, rare that such an item crosses your bows. The Mary Yelloly album was one such item.

The Country Diary of an Edwardian Lady, rediscovered and published in 1977, was greeted with great fanfare and went on to make publishing history. To my mind the Mary Yelloly manuscript is a more interesting animal. I have never come across a document that so viscerally transports you into Austen's world, as this does, through the eyes of a young girl. It speaks of high-ceilinged rooms, of fabulous colour, of governesses, manners, and etiquette. The manuscript goes on to describe long journeys through the English counties, class distinctions, charity, and discipline. The slightly attenuated figures and the interiors, seen through a child's eye, are a delight.

The previous owner of this manuscript was Bryan Hall of the Old Rectory Banningham, in Norfolk, near the Yelloly family's homes. Bryan was an enthusiastic collector of books. His father – the Reverend William Hall, Vicar of Barton Turf – had also been a rabid collector and the house was an overstuffed treasure chest. The collection was not over-funded but its tentacles reached into many areas, from manuscripts to fossils.

Bryan was ailing of health and finance, and the time came for the final dispersal of the contents of Banningham Rectory. A marquee was erected in the adjoining field so that Bryan's rambling and eccentric assemblage could be seen and sold in all its glory. The shame was that Bryan's poor health prevented him from enjoying the occasion as he should have done.

At the view I spotted the Mary Yelloly manuscript within five minutes and from that moment on had eyes for nothing else. Battle commenced, and with the seller's pound of flesh added my initial restraints had been blown to all quarters.

And so Mary and the Grenvilles would go forth, and rightly so. Where they shall go is not up to me. I have played my small part. Within a short time, Charles Miers of Rizzoli International Publications was also hooked on Mary, and the manuscript had found its publisher. Lindsay Stainton, after months of thorough research, brought Mary back to life with the extraordinary story of the Yelloly family. Designer Minnie Weisz brings the delightful illustrations to these pages, and we are fortunate to have the contribution of Helena Bonham Carter.

Sadly, Bryan Hall died last year, leaving what remained of his money to animal causes and churches. He would never know what became of Mary Yelloly and the Grenville family but I am sure he would have approved.

Simon Finch

Introduction

A Picture History of the Grenville Family, a domestic drama in four parts, is the remarkable creation of Mary Yelloly, who was eight years old in 1825 when she began her story, which she told through a series of 256 watercolours, and twelve when she completed it in 1829. As well as being a fictional narrative, it is also a pictorial autobiography, giving us a vivid impression of life in a particular milieu from a child's viewpoint, its very naivety adding a special charm. The *Picture History* depicts the life of an imaginary family, the affluent Grenvilles, their relations and friends, told through the daily activities of their children, which Mary Yelloly based on her own experiences, fusing the imagined and the real worlds she inhabited. Her achievement at such a young age in creating a parallel existence which seems so vivid has an irresistible air of fantasy about it, and opening the album into which the watercolours were later bound we seem to enter her creation without hesitation. The album was labelled 'Miss Mary Yelloly', with a number of contemporary pencil annotations indicating that her mother and sisters had also contributed to her *Picture History*, while a few notes added many years later gave the barest biographical details, stating that she was born in December 1816, that she lived at Carrow Abbey, Norwich, and that she died at the age of only twenty-one in 1838; tantalisingly, nothing more seemed to be known about her or her family.

Modest though these clues were, however, they provided the starting point for unravelling the history of her real life family, and as more detail emerged, it became apparent that Mary's *Picture History* formed part of a sequence begun by her mother in 1797, at the age of twelve or thirteen, which was continued by various children of the family until 1853, when Mrs Yelloly contributed to the last of them, belonging to her granddaughter Anna Maria Suckling. Even more intriguing was the fact that these were all interrelated, each child's *Picture History* apparently relating a different story about the Grenville family, a simple but ingenious literary device that must have developed as Mrs Yelloly, her daughters and in later years, her granddaughter, discussed and evolved the lives of their imaginary subjects. Whether any of the other *Picture Histories* will ever be rediscovered is a tantalising question; we know of their existence only through a memoir by the wife of one of Mrs Yelloly's grandsons, Florence Horatia Nelson Suckling, *A Forgotten Past*, published in 1898[1].

Mary Yelloly's *Picture History* re-emerged at auction in 2004, having belonged to Bryan Hall, an eclectic collector who lived all his life in Norfolk and who had probably acquired it locally, only miles from both the Yellolys' former home in Norwich, and the house in which they lived during the last years of her life, Woodton Hall. This selection of watercolours from Mary's *Picture History* thus allows us a glimpse into her family's life and into the imagination of a young girl.

Mary was born in Finsbury Square, London, on 23 December 1816[2], the ninth of ten children of Dr John Yelloly MD FRS (1774-1842) and his wife Sarah, née Tyssen (1784-1854). Their family perfectly exemplified the emergence of the professional upper middle classes in the early nineteenth century; Mary's father was a distinguished physician[3], and her mother came from a landowning family with extensive properties in Hackney, East London, and in Norfolk. John Yelloly was born in Alnwick, Northumberland, on 30 April 1774, the youngest son and sole survivor of seven children[4]. His father, a merchant, died in 1787 and he was brought up by his mother Jane, née Davison; one of his uncles, Nicholas Davison (1733-1811) was a naval surgeon, while another, Nathaniel Davison (1737-1809), had a more unexpected and exotic career. In 1762 he became secretary and travelling companion to Edward Wortley Montagu (1713-1776), MP, adventurer and criminal, who spent the latter years of his disreputable life abroad[5]. In 1763 Davison accompanied him to Egypt, assisting him in writing up their travels for the Royal Society (although tactfully omitting the more sensational details, such as Montagu's bigamous marriages). On an expedition to the Great Pyramid of Cheops at Giza, Davison made the important discovery of the lowest of a series of five chambers constructed over the king's burial chamber, which still bears his name; subsequently he became the British Consul at Nice and Algiers before returning to England in the late 1770s. The notes and drawings he made in Egypt were bequeathed to his nephew Dr Yelloly, whose widow still owned them at the time of her death in 1854[6].

John Yelloly was educated at Alnwick Grammar School, and then went to Edinburgh to study medicine, perhaps on the advice of his uncle Nicholas, graduating MD in 1796. Edinburgh was one of the leading medical schools of the period, and in Yelloly's day had a particularly strong reputation for medical chemistry, his lifelong interest. On moving to London, he became a licentiate of the Royal College of Physicians in 1800 and in the following year was appointed physician to the General Dispensary, Aldersgate Street, a charitable medical service for the poor of the city established in 1770, and a training ground for young doctors. Not only did he hold progressive medical views, but he also had a social conscience that was evident throughout his life, one of his last publications being *Observations on the Arrangements connected with the Relief of the Sick Poor,* 1837, and it is clear from Mary's *Picture History* that he and his wife instilled their children with a sense of responsibility towards the disadvantaged[7].

Dr Yelloly was ambitious for himself and for the status of his profession[8], and like a number of colleagues, including his Edinburgh contemporary and close friend, the Swiss-born Alexander Marcet (1770-1822)[9], and the Norfolk-born surgeon Astley Cooper (1768-1841)[10], felt increasingly frustrated with the deficiencies both of the Medical Society of London and the Royal College of Physicians. In 1805, Yelloly, Marcet and Cooper were among the prime movers in the establishment of the Medical and Chirurgical Society of London (the forerunner of the Royal Society of Medicine)[11], their chief aim being the exchange of the most up-to-date ideas and practical knowledge. Among their first honorary members was Sir Joseph Banks (1743-1820), President of the Royal Society, through whom John Yelloly must almost certainly have met his future wife, Sarah Tyssen, who was Sir Joseph's ward[12]; they married on 4 August 1806, and a year later, shortly after the birth of their first child, Sarah (who was vaccinated against smallpox by the great Dr Jenner himself), Dr Yelloly was appointed Physician to the London Hospital. By his early thirties, Yelloly had founded a medical society, married an heiress and been appointed to a senior medical post.

Mrs Yelloly came from a wealthy family, the Tyssens, Flemish in origin, who had settled in London in the mid-seventeenth century. Her father, Samuel Tyssen (1755(?)-1800), a distinguished antiquarian and numismatist, had married his cousin Sarah Boddicott in 1782 and they lived at Felix Hall, Kelvedon, Essex, where their two surviving children Sarah (1784-1854) and Samuel (1785-1845) were born, but following his wife's death from consumption in 1790 he could no longer bear to remain there and moved to Narborough Hall, Norfolk, where he died in 1800[13]. His important collection was sold, and the house leased out. Sarah was brought up from 1790 in the care of her maternal grandmother (who died only days after her father) and then by her guardians, one of whom was her father's Administrator, Sir Joseph Banks, whose wife was a cousin of the Tyssens[14]. In 1797, when she was twelve or thirteen, she began what her grandson's wife Mrs Suckling described as an illustrated play or romance (still in the family's possession in 1898), which she completed in 1803 or 5, composed of a series of watercolours illustrating a story of youthful love, partly set in a house reminiscent of Narborough Hall[15], which must be regarded as the progenitor of the *Picture Histories* that were to become an important feature of her family's life. As a girl, Mrs Yelloly had had drawing lessons, which was usual for young ladies of her background, and became a very accomplished artist; she was said to have been taught by a leading watercolourist of the day, perhaps, although the chronology makes it unlikely, by Copley Fielding[16], a stalwart of the Society of Painters in Water-Colours, founded in 1804. Certainly her serious interest in watercolour was to continue throughout her life, an enthusiasm that she was to pass onto her children.

As Jane Austen suggested in *Northanger Abbey*, 1818, the ability to draw and paint had become the norm for those who aspired to refined taste; her heroine Catherine Morland, the unsophisticated daughter of a country clergyman, 'declared she would give anything in the world to be able to draw…she was heartily ashamed of her ignorance' as she listened to Henry Tilney and his sister Eleanor 'viewing the country with the eyes of persons accustomed to drawing, and decided on its capability of being formed into pictures with all the eagerness of real taste. Here Catherine was quite lost. She knew nothing of drawing – nothing of taste'. Professional artists were not slow to capitalise on this fashionable pastime, publishing instruction manuals as well as endorsing ranges of paper, paints, brushes and so on: 'Painting has long been considered as a graceful accomplishment for the dignified and opulent, and also a useful acquirement for those who compose the middle ranks of society', noted the introduction to one of these numerous drawing books[17]. For some, accomplishments such as drawing were a form of social advancement, perhaps even a way of attracting a husband. In *Pride and Prejudice*, 1813, however, the snobbish Miss Bingley dismisses such superficial graces: '"no one can be really esteemed accomplished, who does not greatly surpass what is usually met with. . . A woman must have a thorough knowledge of music, singing, drawing, dancing and the modern languages, to deserve the word; and beside all this, she must possess a certain something in her air and manner"… "All this she must possess", added Darcy, "and to all this she must yet add something more substantial, in the improvement of her mind by extensive reading."' As Elizabeth Bennet wryly noted, such high expectations were unlikely to be fulfilled by many women. Perhaps the future Mrs Yelloly, with her rather serious approach to life, might have had some claims to being considered a 'really accomplished woman'.

Following their marriage in 1806, Dr and Mrs Yelloly settled in Finsbury Square. They were to have ten children: Sarah Boddicott

(1807-1896), Jane Davison (1808-1838), John (1809-1892), who became a clergyman, Harriet (1810-1858), Sophia Mary (1811-1840), Samuel Tyssen (1812-1860), who became a lawyer, Nicholas Nathaniel (1814-1836), Anna Maria (1815-1880), Mary (1816-1838) and Eleanor Margaret (1820-1860). To judge from Dr Yelloly's will, first drafted in 1826[18], in which he noted that 'we have spent twenty years of our lives very happily together', he also had considerable respect for his wife's 'judgement, rectitude and discrimination…every year gives me more reason to respect and admire her sound judgement, her high sense of honour, the independence and integrity of her character'. Inevitably, Mrs Yelloly's chief responsibility lay in the upbringing of their large family, while Dr Yelloly pursued his career as a senior physician at the London Hospital and as an active member of the Medical and Chirurgical Society of London, establishing its library and contributing articles to its journal, ranging from a description of a case of paralysis caused by a tumour of the brain, 1809, to a paper on a novel procedure for the removal of bladder stone, 1815, this being an anticipation of his important work at Norwich. In 1814, he was elected a Fellow of the Royal Society, with the support of Dr Marcet, Sir Joseph Banks and Sir Astley Cooper. Then, in June 1818, apparently because of his wife's ill-health, he resigned his post at the London Hospital, and the family moved to Norwich (not far from Mrs Yelloly's brother, Samuel Tyssen, at Narborough Hall), perhaps at the invitation of Alexander and Jane Marcet's friend, a well-known local surgeon, Philip Meadows Martineau, the uncle of the future famous writer, feminist and abolitionist, Harriet Martineau (1802-1876). The Yellolys rented Carrow Abbey, their home until 1833, from the Martineau family[19], and they must certainly have known Harriet as a young woman.

Norfolk was known in medical circles for its unusually high incidence of bladder stone; the county hospital held a collection of over 1500 stones removed from patients since 1771 (in the pre-anaesthesia age, an extremely painful procedure), and both Alexander Marcet and John Yelloly had a longstanding interest in the chemical composition of these stones, hoping to discover the causes of the complaint and thus a possible remedy. Yelloly, who was appointed physician to the Norfolk and Norwich Hospital in 1821, undertook the study of the epidemiology and chemical analysis of these stones, the results being published by the Royal Society in 1829-1830[20]. Although he probably forfeited advancement to the highest professional distinctions when he left London for Norwich, his work anticipated the rapid developments in medical chemistry, pathology and physiology that followed later in the century.

A Picture History of the Grenville Family by Mary Yelloly

In the meantime, his large family was growing up at Carrow Abbey. The Yelloly household was run on fairly strict lines. A nurse took care of the children when they were young, and the family employed a French governess, Mlle. de Yeux, but Mrs Yelloly herself supervised the schoolroom, devising a curriculum that emphasised self-discipline, hard work and reward for virtue. Temper, disobedience and idleness – described by the educationalist Hannah More as 'the root of all evil in children' – brought their inevitable punishment, usually exclusion from visits to their parents after dinner. Sad little notes recorded failures; Sarah, the eldest child, aged nine, wrote to her 'Dear Dear Mama' to apologise for failing to prepare her lessons on time and for losing her temper [21]. Although the boys went to school, the girls were educated at home. The Yellolys were close friends of Dr Alexander Marcet and his wife Jane, who was the author of several influential and best-selling books that aimed to explain economics and science to children (Michael Faraday credited her with introducing him to electrochemistry) – indeed Dr Yelloly himself had helped her to edit *Conversations on Chemistry*, 1805 [22] – but their own children's education seems to have been rather more conventional. Certainly when they were very young, their journals and a timetable drawn up by Mrs Yelloly reveal the usual fare of reading, writing, arithmetic, French, geography and music, underpinned by piety. Hannah More had noted that women's 'knowledge is not like the learning of men, to be reproduced in some literary composition nor *ever* in any learned profession, but is to come out in conduct', and Mrs Yelloly's foremost concern seems to have been to ensure that her daughters should be both virtuous as well as accomplished, and become good wives and mothers.

However, what made Mrs Yelloly's system of education somewhat different was her interest in drawing as an educational medium. This had been advocated by Rousseau and taken up by Maria Edgeworth among others, the rationale being that children would learn best if education were made amusing and pleasurable. It is perhaps in this context that the Yelloly children's *Picture Histories* should be seen. Leading a comparatively isolated and austere existence (certainly by today's standards), the children were dependent on their own resources for entertaining themselves. At exactly the same time that Mary Yelloly was devising her *Picture History*, the young Brontë children (Charlotte, like Mary, was born in 1816), living in their father's remote parsonage at Haworth, were creating their imaginary worlds of Angria and Gondal, and their writing could switch from everyday life to the imagined world and back again in a single sentence; a generation earlier, at the age of fourteen, Jane Austen had written her first novel *Love and Friendship*, 1790. This is not

to claim that the Yellolly children's inventions could or should be compared with these, but simply to suggest that they grew from much the same impetus. Jane Austen's comment in a letter of 1814 that '3 or 4 families in a Country Village is the very thing to work on' could also sum up the subject matter explored by the Yellolys in their *Picture Histories*. Mary herself must have had a precocious imagination to invent her story, as well as considerable skill and patience as a watercolourist to illustrate it so exquisitely. Although there must have been many other families whose children amused themselves and their parents by devising illustrated stories or simply by recording incidents from their daily lives, surprisingly few seem to have survived from this period. An exception is the group of drawings made by the children of the banker Andrew Drummond in the late 1820s, at the same time as the Yellolys were compiling their *Picture Histories*. The Drummonds' watercolours, preserved together with poems, essays and letters by a cousin, reveal a very similar existence to that depicted by Mary Yelloly – life in a large modern country house – where the seven children and their cousins made their own amusements when they were not working hard in the schoolroom[23]. The Yellolys' particular originality, however, lay in transforming their everyday existence into fictional narrative.

The routine of provincial life was enlivened by the family's annual visits to London, several of which were described in some detail by the Yellolys' eldest daughter Sarah in her journal[24]. There they met old friends, saw the sights and visited the fashionable shops in Bond Street, went to the opera and the theatre, and to the annual exhibition of the Watercolour Society, a particular interest of Mrs Yelloly's ever since their exhibitions had begun in 1805. They also took the opportunity of visiting the artists' suppliers, Rowney's, in order to stock up on watercolours and paper. Writing in 1898, Mrs Suckling noted that each girl kept an album and described the *Picture History of the Grenville Family who reside at Woodlands Hall* begun in 1825 by Anna Maria, who was a year older than Mary, but she seems to have been unaware of Mary's own *Picture History of the Grenville Family of Rosedale House and Woodlands Hall*, also begun in 1825 (perhaps by 1898 it had already left the family, or had been put away in a cupboard years before)[25]. The stories seem to have been distinct, but the characters overlapped, and all Anna Maria and Mary's older sisters and their mother contributed drawings to each other's albums. The aristocratic-sounding Grenvilles and their numerous relations were doubtless based on the Yelloly and Tyssen families, but with a touch of girlish fantasy they are made just a little more glamorous (here one is reminded of *The Young*

Visitors, 1890, written by Daisy Ashford when she was nine). The Yellolys' tours to the north of England, where they had cousins, and to Scotland, in their primrose-yellow carriage, which was in use until the 1850s, provided the inspiration for many of the children's drawings: in Mary's *Picture History* there is a section devoted to a tour to the Highlands, as well as another to the west country, and the Grenvilles' yellow carriage is a familiar sight. It made its last appearance in the *Picture History* devised by Anna Maria Suckling (daughter of Anna Maria Yelloly) in 1853, when it carried Charles Grenville and Maria Flemmington (spelt by Mary as 'Fennington' or 'Fennenton') – both of whom are introduced to us in Mary's *Picture History* – from their wedding and on their honeymoon[26].

Reality and fantasy were also combined in Mary's views of interiors, which must again have been based on the homes of her friends and family. Although the Yellolys' house was mediaeval in origin, the Grenvilles live in modern houses, and the furnishings are in keeping; by the early nineteenth century, home life had become an important part of one's social identity, and the desire for increasingly comfortable surroundings was encouraged by the lavish illustrations to such aspirational furnishing and decorative publications as Rudolph Ackermann's pioneering *Repository of Arts*, published monthly between 1809 and 1828, which showed all the most fashionable developments in interior design, furniture and fashion. Mary Yelloly's lovingly detailed depiction of elaborate window hangings, for instance, reflects the influence of these publications. By the early nineteenth century, a growing sense of informality had become noticeable in English houses, a derangé quality such as that noted by Jane Austen in *Persuasion*, 1818, where the Elliott sisters visiting the Musgroves in the old-fashioned square parlour at Uppercross found 'the present daughters of the house giving the proper air of confusion by a grand pianoforte and a harp, flower stands and little tables placed in every direction'. Mary Yelloly's watercolours illustrate this change, and are a mine of information on the details of life in well-to-do households, such as the decoration of the walls, the height at which paintings were hung, the use of fitted carpets with contrasting borders as well as those with rather alarming overall patterns [27], and the arrangement of furniture in each room [28]; several tables, chairs, and bookcases recur throughout the *Picture History*, suggesting that they were real objects in the Yelloly household. Following the rapid growth of interest in landscaping and gardening in the previous century, nature no longer seemed threatening but positively enjoyable, so that country houses were built with large sash windows, often down to the ground, designed to frame the view for the pleasure of those inside, while flowering plants displayed in stands and vases of cut flowers were used as never before, establishing a taste that was to become ever more popular[29]. Mary Yelloly's *Picture History* includes numerous details of this sort, and also introduces us to the housekeepers' rooms in the Grenvilles' houses (although never to the kitchens), as well to the children's bedrooms, nurseries and schoolrooms.

The landscape watercolours in the *Picture History* are of a type reasonably familiar from the albums of adult amateurs of the period, but are given added interest because they sustain the narrative flow of the story and because they are surprisingly accomplished to have been painted by a young child, even if on occasion she was helped by a sister or by her mother. The family's serious interest in the work of professional watercolourists is apparent from their annual visits to exhibitions in London, and Mrs Yelloly herself was sufficiently skilled to be able to teach her children to paint. As Rudolf Ackermann had noted in 1810, 'Drawing, the ground-work of refined taste in the arts, is now considered and very justly, as an indispensable requisite in the education of both sexes. In that of females in particular, it has opened a prodigious field of the excursions of imagination, invention and ingenuity'. Many of the landscapes in the *Picture History* must have been inspired by plates in drawing manuals produced by well-known artists to capitalise on the fashionable interest in watercolours, those by John Varley (1778-1842) and the young David Cox (1783-1859) almost certainly being the Yellolys' chief models [30]; some of the Lake District views were probably inspired by T. H. Fielding's handsome folio, *Cumberland, Westmoreland and Lancashire Illustrated*, 1822, a copy of which was owned by Mrs Yelloly [31].

Remarkably, Mary Yelloly sustained the creation of her *Picture History* over the course of four years, a significant achievement for a young child, suggesting either considerable self-discipline or perhaps a mother determined to encourage such a virtue in her daughter. Although we know that she kept a journal into the 1830s, this has not survived, and her short life remains mysterious once she had finished her story of the Grenvilles in 1829. In 1832, her father retired from the Norfolk and Norwich Hospital and the family moved to Woodton Hall [32], a handsome house some ten miles away, which they rented from the Suckling family (close relations of Admiral Horatio Nelson, whose mother was Catherine Suckling); in 1840 Mary's sister Anna Maria (1815-1880) was to marry Robert Suckling. Two watercolours of the interior of Woodton Hall by Harriet Yelloly (1810-1858), one showing the drawing room in 1835 with two of the girls, one of whom is painting, seem to be the only surviving visual evidence of their life there [33], although another *Picture History* apparently included many views of the house and its environs [34]. In 1836, Nicholas Yelloly became the first of the family to die from consumption, at the age of twenty-two. Mary had probably begun to develop consumption at the beginning of 1838; certainly when her brother John (by now a clergyman) came home that spring, suffering from a mild attack of smallpox, her parents decided that in her already weakened state she must be removed from the possibility of infection, and she was sent to stay with her brother Sam, a lawyer in Ipswich. In the meantime, Jane, Harriet and Anna all contracted smallpox, and on 21 June, Jane died, aged thirty. On the following day, Mary herself died, apparently from the shock of her journey when she was already seriously ill with consumption. The deaths of two sisters on consecutive days must have been a terrible blow to the family, made even more difficult to bear by the fact that within months Sophia became ill with consumption, dying in January 1840 at the age of twenty-eight [35].

In 1839, the Yellolys' lease of Woodton Hall came to an end, and the family moved to Cavendish Hall in Suffolk the following year. There Dr Yelloly died in 1842, having been unwell since an accident in 1840 and the subsequent paralysis he suffered. Mrs Yelloly died in 1854[36], Harriet in 1858 and Samuel in 1860, both from consumption. Their sister Eleanor, the youngest of the family, who had married their cousin John Tyssen, also died in 1860 and Anna Maria Suckling in 1880. In 1892, the Rev. John Yelloly died and finally Sarah, the eldest of the Yelloly children, died in 1896. All the members of the family are commemorated in the church at Woodton, Norfolk, but Mary Yelloly's *Picture History,* although fictional in intent, is unquestionably the most engaging glimpse into their childhood to have survived.

A Picture History

OF THE

Grenville Family
Vol 1

BEGUN

AUGUST 1825

Mary Yelloly

Mary Yelloly's *Picture History of the Grenville Family* is composed of four volumes, which were bound together after her death in 1838. This, the first, was begun in 1825, when she was only 8 years old, and completed the following year. To judge from the obviously adult handwriting, it was probably her mother who wrote the title page, and she – or perhaps an older sister – who inscribed many of the titles beneath the watercolours (following the style of contemporary engravings), and listed the chief *dramatis personae*: Mr and Mrs Grenville, Miss Beaufort, governess, and their four children, Eleanor, 8 (the same age as Mary Yelloly), Augusta, 7, Maria Louisa, 3, and Charles, 'an infant'.

We are introduced to the family and their homes, Rosedale House in Gloucestershire and Woodlands Hall, and follow the children through their daily routines, which mirror those of the young Yellolys, as we know from the journals they kept. Many of the watercolours throughout the album are annotated in pencil – again, almost certainly by Mrs Yelloly – indicating their authorship; the great majority are by Mary, but all her elder sisters as well as her brother Nicholas contributed. Unlike subsequent instalments, there is no introductory narrative to the first volume, which opens with a view of Rosedale House (25), by Sophia Yelloly (who was 14) and Mama,

showing a typically simple but handsome Georgian country house set in parkland, doubtless based on many known to the Yelloly family. A number of other more modest houses are included, ranging from the handsome old dower house in which Mr Grenville's mother lived near Woodlands Hall (37) to a farm on the estate (44) and a cottage in the park at Rosedale (27), complete with bee-skeps, where an old servant of the family lives, the aptly named Mrs Tidy. Falkoner Court (45), the home of the children's friend Miss Stanley, is identified with an endearingly smudged and laboured description, probably written by Mary herself. The family is shown setting off on one of the journeys that they make throughout the *Picture History* in a yellow carriage (32), which in real life belonged to the Yelloly family and was used by them until 1853, either to travel between their houses or to visit friends and relations. Several views in the Lake District, including 'Clearburn Lake' (33) – Mary used both real and, as here, invented place-names – suggest that the Grenvilles went to visit the wealthy relation from whom they were later to inherit Bellemere Park, Cumberland. Subsequently, the family enjoys a holiday by the sea, which had become fashionable since around 1800, including a boating trip for the children with a 'naval officer friend' (34) as well as walks along the shore with Mama (35). At home, the children are taken on carriage rides by their father, the only occasions on which a male presence is apparent, to visit friends or their grandmother (42), go for walks (26, 36) and take messages for their parents (44). An important element in the subsequent development of the *Picture History* is introduced with the view of the Rev. George Melville's rectory (46); in the next volume, he is to marry the children's governess, Miss Beaufort. The last illustration shows Mrs Grenville watering the flowers at Rosedale House (47).

Compared with preceding generations, the children depicted by Mary Yelloly enjoyed a much less formalised way of life; Mrs Grenville enjoys her children's company and spends a good deal of time with them, allowing them to let off their high spirits in walks and games, while still expecting good behaviour. The increased sense of freedom was also apparent in more informal and comfortable clothes that were then fashionable. The ideal look for women was streamlined, so the narrow-cut dresses had high waists, sloping shoulders and close-fitting sleeves, with short jackets (known as spencers), and the ever essential hat when in the country, generally straw. Their undergarments were much less restricting than they had been in the previous century or would be by the 1850s. Children's dresses generally followed adult styles, although they were shorter in length and little girls wore pantaloons, as Mary so charmingly depicts.

The watercolours of interiors, especially in the first volume, reflect the difficulty of conveying a sense of relative scale, but this only adds to the unmistakably child's-eye impression of life: whether dancing (38-9), or playing shuttlecock in the nursery (40) or talking to one another in their bedroom (31), the children are often dwarfed by the furniture, as if, like Alice in Wonderland, they have swallowed some magic potion. The family's houses are modern, furnished and decorated in contemporary style. The high-ceilinged regular-shaped rooms and tall sash windows, through which light comes in freely, contrast both with previous architectural styles and with the succeeding Victorian period, when the very sparseness of the interiors shown here would have seemed hopelessly old-fashioned. From the outset, we are aware of a family whose homes reflect an awareness of changing fashions in interior design, yet without ever appearing too modish, and although this is supposedly the imaginary world of the Grenvilles, we can be fairly sure that Mary Yelloly is observing and recording the real world in which she lived.

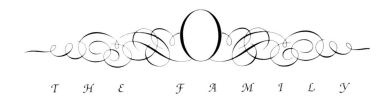

T H E   F A M I L Y

MR & MRS GRENVILLE
MISS BEAUFORT THE GOVERNESS

A N D

T H E I R   C H I L D R E N

ELEANOR   *8 years*

AUGUSTA   *7 years*

MARIA LOUISA   *3 years*

CHARLES   *an infant*

OF

ROSEDALE HOUSE & WOODLANDS HALL

Rosedale House

Avenue at Rosedale
Nurse. Agusta, and Maria. Lousa.

Mrs Tidy's cottage at Rosedale
Nurse & Maria Louisa

Mrs Grenville's sitting room
Mrs G. Eleanor & Augusta

Miss Beauforts Room Roseda.
Nurse Augusta's Maria Louisa

Nursery Bed room Rosedale
Miss Eleanor Augusta. Mrs Grenville & Maid.

Elleanor & Augusta's room.

Elleanor, Augusta & Anna Louisa

The Grenvilles going a Journey.
Mr & Mrs Grenville Eleanor & Augusta.

View near Clearburn Lake
Mr Grenville & Eleanor

Coast Scene

Eleanor Augusta & Mr Benson

a Naval Officer friend of the Grenvill

Coast Scene

Near Woodlands

Mrs Grenville Eleanor & Augusta

Grenville House residence of Mr Grenville's mother

Drawing room.

Eleanor & Agusta dancing. Caroline Grenville
their cousin, who goes to school 1½ mile from Woodlands &
the piano Forte

Sitting room Woodlands
Eleanor & Augusta
practising their dancing.

Nursery Woodlands Hall

Augusta and Maria Jennenton

Grenville House.
Eleanor with her Mamma,

Mr and Mrs Grenville

Turnpike on the road.

44

Farm at Rosedale
Augusta taking a message
to Mrs Farley the farmer's wife.

Falkner Court garden front
Eleanor, Maria Louisa, and
Miss Stanley

46

Rev.ᵈ George Melviles rear Villa House

South view of Rosedale House,
Mrs. Grenville watering her flowers.

A

Picture History

OF THE

GRENVILLE FAMILY

Vol 2

BEGUN

AUGUST 1826

 Mary Yelloly

Volume 2 was begun by Mary in August 1826, when she was nine and a half years old, and completed the following July. The imaginary Grenville children, however, have grown up more rapidly: Eleanor is now 12, Augusta, 11, Maria Louisa, 7, Charles, 5, and there are two further additions to the family, Sophia Agnes, 3, and Henry Theodore, 1. A short narrative introduces the pictures, and one can imagine Mary and her siblings discussing the unfolding story with their mother. While Mama had been responsible for most of the descriptive titles in the first volume, Mary carefully wrote many of those in this volume herself, complete with occasional spelling errors.

The Grenville family continue to live at Rosedale House and Woodlands Hall; the children's governess, Miss Beaufort, marries the Rev. George Melville, and is shown holding her first baby outside Pleasant Farm, the home of her parents-in-law (53); her younger sister, Miss Caroline Beaufort, joins the household as the new governess. The chief event that carries forward the narrative of this volume is the fortuitous inheritance, following the death of a distant relation, of 'a large estate, & fine house…Bellemere Park' (60), in the Lake District, 'including the presentation to the Rectory', in which Mr and Mrs Melville are duly installed (59). The Grenvilles set off to stay at their new property (which

bears some resemblance to Felix Hall, Essex, Mrs Yellory's birthplace), and we are introduced to the house and the neighbourhood (58, 60, 64), including the nearby Mount Cathedral (81), which looks much like Norwich Cathedral, only moments from the Yellolys' home. There are several accomplished landscapes of Lake District views (58, 80) – an area which the Yellory family themselves regularly visited – probably inspired by plates in publications like T. H. Fielding's Cumberland, Westmorland and Lancashire Illustrated, 1822, of which Mrs Yellory owned a copy.

A theme that recurs throughout the album, and which doubtless mirrored the Yellolys' real lives, is the responsibility the children are encouraged to take for the welfare of their poorer neighbours. Mrs Grenville concerns herself with these matters throughout the Picture History, encouraging her children by her own example. Eleanor and Augusta count their savings with a view to buying a new work-box, but decide instead to spend the money on cloth to make garments for the poor (62); they ask their mother to allow them to buy the material (63), while Maria Louisa and Sophia forego fruit in order to give it to the mother of their poor friend Mary Price, to whom Augusta and her cousin Louisa Harcourt also present several of their own dolls (71, 73). Mrs Grenville, together with her girls, visits the poor of the neighbourhood to distribute food and clothes and to read to the elderly Mrs Sandby in her quaint old cottage

(76-7), and to inspect the school the family has established, as well as making arrangements with Mrs Melville for the care of the sick and aged in her absence (78). In one of the most striking images, Mrs Grenville and one of her daughters are shown standing by a table in the housekeeper's room at Bellemere, which is laden with joints of meat for distribution to the poor (65). Other activities, however, are not omitted: lessons with Mama, in the schoolroom and the governess's room (61, 70), and church on Sundays (64), as well as visits to neighbours and walks around Lake Bellemere (60,66), which like many other locations depicted in the album is given a fictional name. The volume ends as Mrs Grenville becomes ill (74-5) – perhaps a reflection of Mrs Yelloly's own real-life illness - and the younger children are therefore dispatched in the care of Miss Beaufort to Hill House, the home of their maternal grandmother, Lady Delville, where they are later joined (Volume 3) by the rest of the family when Mrs Grenville has recovered.

Throughout the *Picture History*, schoolrooms feature prominently. Mary Yelloly must have based these scenes on her own and her siblings' education, which her mother supervised with great care. A descendant, Mrs Suckling, transcribed the instructions Mrs Yelloly had drawn up some years earlier, from which this is a short extract: 'The rule of the day, as laid down in their mother's own hand, was as follows:

Monday, Tuesday, etc

To walk for an hour and a half after breakfast, at the expiration of that time the school bell to be rung, everyone to come in and go to lessons in the following manner:-

Sarah to teach Sophia to read; in the meantime Sam to write and sum, Sophia to do the same whilst Sam reads.

During this time Harriet to teach the little ones, and Jane to do long division sums.'

Mary's *Picture History* reveals an imaginary family living in privileged circumstances, but it also reflects her own life, a well-to-do, ordered and self-disciplined existence, shaped above all by her mother's insistence on modesty, thrift, obedience, godliness and practical consideration for those less fortunate, affirming the primacy of the domestic sphere and the role of women within it.

T H E   F A M I L Y

MR & MRS GRENVILLE
MISS BEAUFORT THE GOVERNESS

A N D

T H E I R   C H I L D R E N

ELEANOR *12 years*

AUGUSTA *11 years*

MARIA LOUISA *7 years*

CHARLES *5 years*

SOPHIA AGNES *3 years*

HENRY THEODORE *1 years*

OF

R O S E D A L E   H O U S E   &   W O O D L A N D S   H A L L

Pleasant Farm residence of Mr Willm Melville where Mr & Mrs Geo Melville are staying

Mrs Geo Melville late Miss Beaufort
walking out near Gayflower
with Maria Louisa Charles Grenville

Distant view of old Mrs Sandy
Cottage Mrs Grenville Eleonor & Augusta
taking her the fruit &c which they had saved

Nursery Rosedale Eleanor & Augusta

Mrs Grenvilles sitting room Rosedale
Mrs Grenville & Eleanor cutting out

Bettemere Lake

Rectory Bellemere

Bellemere Park
Residence of Mr & Mrs Grenville
lately left them by a distant relation

School Room Bellemere

Eleanor & Augusta's Room. Bellemere

Mrs Grenville's sitting room

Mrs Grenville Eleanor

as Mrs G wished to speak to Mrs Melville about
a person in the neighbourhood who was ill

Housekeeper's room Bellemere
Mrs Grenville giving directions to the
housekeeper relative to distributing the

Drawing room Rectory
Eleanor and Augusta Charles Nurse and baby

Mrs Melvilles bedroom Rectory

Sleeping room attic's Bellemere
Eleanor writing to Miss Delville

Dressing room east end Bellevue
now used as a sitting room for

Miss Beauforts room

Miss Beaufort hearing Maria Louisa her lessons

Nursery Bellemere Maria Louisa Sophia

Dressing room Bellemere

Sleeping room attics Bellemen

Mr Grenville's sitting room
Elleanor reading to Mrs Grenville who is very ill

Mrs Grenville's bedroom

Augusta and Mrs Grenville who is better

Mr Grenville calling on & reading

Mrs Grenville & Eleanor going
round the village of Bellemere to visit
their poor neighbours previous to

Mrs Grenville's sitting room

Bellemere Mrs G & Mrs Melleville consulting about the sick
caged in the neighbourhood & Mrs G leaving the sum for relief
during their absence with Mrs M

Eleanor & Augusta's room Bellemere

Cottage Farm Bellemere

81

Mount Cathedral about 5 miles from Bellemere

A

Picture History

OF THE

GRENVILLE FAMILY

Vol 3

BEGUN

AUGUST 1827

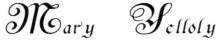

Mary Yelloly

Volume 3 is undated, but from the ages of the Grenville children and the dates of Volumes 2 and 4 it is apparent that Mary worked on this in 1827-8, between the ages of 10 and 11. By now, Eleanor Grenville is 13, Augusta, 12, Maria Louisa, 8, Charles, 6, Sophia Agnes, 4, and Henry Theodore, 2. Miss Caroline Beaufort remains their governess, and the family continues to live at Rosedale House, Woodlands Hall and Bellemere Park.

At the start of this volume, the family is staying with Mrs Grenville's mother, Lady Delville, of Hill House (87), whose daughter-in-law Lady Delville Jr. is also a visitor, with her new baby (88). While at her grandmother's house, Maria Louisa welcomes a newly arrived guest, Miss Stanley, and the two little girls are shown in the sitting-room, with its fashionable Soane-inspired furniture, the chandelier (perhaps bagged to protect it from dust) reflected in the overmantel glass (89). One of the most delightful watercolours in this volume shows Eleanor and Augusta playing with their 'kittons', which they must have taken home to Rosedale, for they subsequently reappear as slightly older and more mischievous creatures (90, 96). The Grenvilles then return to Rosedale for about six weeks, where the children's lessons resume (baby Henry looks on from his high-chair) (97); Nurse and Sophia are shown in the housekeeper's room (100), Miss Melville calls, during a visit to her grandparents at Pleasant Farm (96), and their cousin Miss Delville also visits them (101) before the family sets off for Woodlands. Their journey, in the familiar primrose-yellow carriage, through a wild and romantic landscape, complete with an ancient castle, is shown (102), followed by their arrival at Woodlands Hall (103) where they stay for several months, their domestic routine there being illustrated; Mrs Grenville and Augusta visit an elderly villager, Maria Louisa helps her mother arrange clothes in her dressing room, Mrs Grenville reads in her elegant boudoir and the younger children have dinner in the nursery (105, 110-12). While there, Mr Weston, 'an opulent miller' (104) near the village of Burnside (107) 'proposes an alliance for his eldest son [a farmer] with Miss Caroline Beaufort, which is accepted with the approbation of all parties'. Although the Picture History is the work of a child (albeit with a good deal of adult input), the social distinctions of early nineteenth-century society are carefully (if unconsciously) observed, for while it would never have done for a Miss Grenville to marry a miller's son, however prosperous, it is perfectly appropriate for their governess Caroline Beaufort to do so. This recalls Jane Austen's eponymous heroine Emma Woodhouse, who in her determination to advance the social standing of a young protégée initially attempted to prevent her from accepting an offer of marriage from an eligible young farmer as being beneath her.

The volume ends with the Grenvilles going on an extensive tour, as had become extremely fashionable for the well-to-do, from Rosedale in Gloucestershire to Cornwall, then to Kent and up to Norfolk, before zigzagging across the Midlands and into North Wales, and then northwards to Cheshire, Yorkshire and Westmorland, concluding at Bellemere in Cumberland, their route being shown on a carefully drawn map (114), an ingenious and enjoyable way of giving a geography lesson to Mary Yelloly and her younger siblings, combining the fictitious narrative of the Grenvilles with reality. Indeed, while the map indicates the Grenvilles' fictitious houses, the Yellolys' real homes are also marked, and the final watercolours in this volume are views of their villa in Epping Forest, for some years their summer residence (117), Carrow Abbey, Norwich (116), their home throughout the years when Mary was compiling this *Picture History*, and Narborough Hall (118), about thirty-five miles away, owned by her maternal uncle Samuel Tyssen (1785-1845), where her mother had spent part of her childhood, this watercolour probably being based on John Sell Cotman's engraved view of the house for *Excursions in Norfolk*, 1819.

    Mary Yelloly's developing ability as an artist is apparent from the landscapes in the volume (92, 115), which suggest that, like her mother and elder sisters, she was by now aware of contemporary artists like John Varley, Copley Fielding and David Cox among others, whether from having seen original watercolours by them – the Yellolys certainly visited the London exhibitions of the Society of Painters in Watercolour, as we know from Sarah's journal – or from studying their illustrated drawing manuals that became so popular from around 1800. The picturesque tour made by the Grenvilles was almost certainly based on reality, since Mary's niece recorded many years later that the Yellolys themselves went on such journeys in their old yellow carriage, as far afield as Scotland (where the Grenvilles go in Volume 4), stopping where they pleased for a few days to make sketches and visiting Dr Yelloly's Northumbrian cousins en route to the Lake District.

T H E   F A M I L Y

MR & MRS GRENVILLE
MISS BEAUFORT THE GOVERNESS

AND

THEIR CHILDREN

ELEANOR   13 years

AUGUSTA   12 years

MARIA LOUISA   8 years

CHARLES   6 years

SOPHIA AGNES   4 years

HENRY THEODORE   2 years

OF

ROSEDALE HOUSE, WOODLANDS HALL &
BELLEMERE PARK

Hill House East Front

Residence of Lady Delville Sen.

Library Hill House.
Lady Delville Jun.ʳ and her Baby

Sitting Room D

Maria Louisa and Miss Stanley

Hampton Lodge

Mrs Hurtons residence

Lady Delville's Sitting Room
Eleanor and Augusta playing their Kittens

Cottage near Hill House

The Grenvilles on their way from Hill Place to Rosedale.

Distant View of Meretown
where the Grenvilles spend a week.

Scene between Hill House

and Rosedale

Mrs Grenville's Sitting Room
Miss Melville who is come to
stay a little while with her grand-papa and Louisa

School Room Rosedale

Miss Beaufort Maria Louisa Sophia and Henry

Farm in Grounds at Rosedale

Mr Auberry's House

Housekeeper's Room

Rosedale. The Housekeeper Nurse and Sophia

Spare Room Rosedale

Eleanor Augusta and Miss Delville who is staying

The Grenvilles on their
way from Prosedale to Woodlands

Woodlands Hall

The Grenvilles arrive there

Mr Weston's Mill

at Burnside near Woodlands

Mrs G and Augusta

Mr Weston Sen

Village of Burnside

Hall at Woodlands
Mrs Grenville.

Mrs G's Dressing Room
Mrs G and Maria Louisa

Mrs G's Dressing Room
Mrs G and Maria Louisa

Nursery Woodlands

Maria Louisa Sophia Charles & Henry having

Mrs Grenville's Boudoir

Dining Room

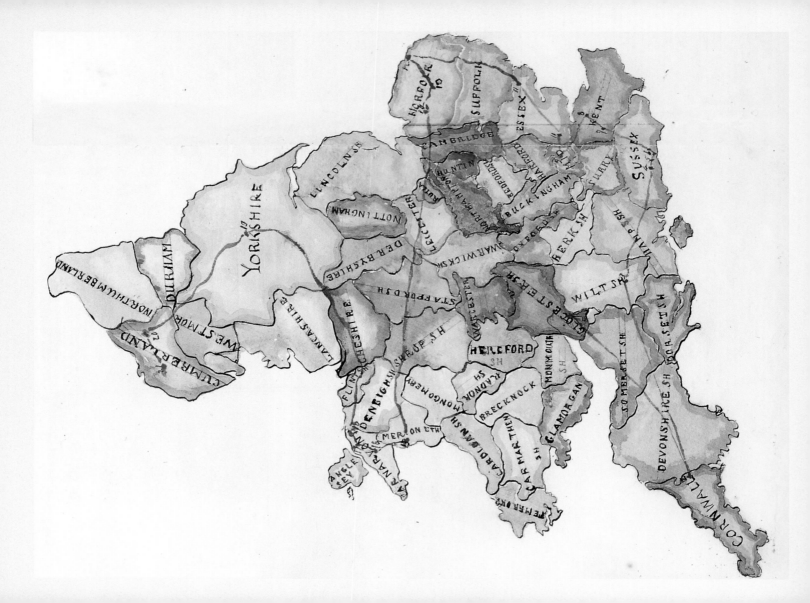

Harlech Castle

Carrow Abbey, near Norwich

House on Epping Forest

Narburgh Hall Norfolk

A Picture History

OF THE

GRENVILLE FAMILY

Vol 4

BEGUN

AUGUST 1828

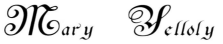

Mary Yelloly

The last part of Mary Yelloly's *Picture History* was begun on 6 August 1828 and completed in August 1829, when she was twelve and a half years old. Eleanor Grenville is now 14, Augusta, 13, Maria Louisa, 9, Charles, 7, Sophia Agnes, 5, and Henry Theodore is 3. Miss Caroline Beaufort is still governess to the children, but in the course of this volume marries Mr Weston, a prosperous young farmer; the family continue to divide their time between their three houses.

Although the introductory text is still written by Mama, all the descriptions beneath the watercolours seem to be in Mary's hand. Her compositions have become considerably more sophisticated since she began her *Picture History* in 1825; she is able to judge relative scale much better, to handle perspective, light and shade with considerable ease, and to place figures convincingly in her designs, while the family practice of contributing to one another's albums is continued, with a number of watercolours by her sisters or Mama. From at least 1828, when she began this final volume of her *Picture History*, Mary was also required to keep a daily journal, like her older sisters, in which she noted her activities hour by hour: prayers, arithmetic, reading, writing, French, piano duets with her music teacher, sewing, poetry recitation, walks and so on. All this was reflected in her depictions of the imaginary Grenville family.

At the start of this volume, the Grenvilles are staying at Bellemere Park (123), the grandest of their houses, which Mr Grenville had inherited several years earlier from a distant relation. The younger girls are shown in the school room (126), and in another scene, one of them (perhaps Sophia) touchingly presents Mrs Grenville with 'a flower of her own raising' (130). Later in the volume, Sophia is taken by Nurse for a donkey ride along the shore of Lake Bellemere (141), and Maria Louisa and Sophia feed their 'tame chickhaens' (140). Mr and Mrs Fennington of Villa House near Rosedale (127) come to stay, bringing their three children; according to Mary Yelloly's niece, this subplot in her narrative was taken up in one of the very last of the family's *Picture Histories*, compiled in 1850-3, when Miss Fennington married Charles Grenville, who would by then have been in his early thirties. At the Rectory, Mrs Melville (the children's former governess) has a new baby (128), and when her sister marries Mr Weston and the bridal couple go to visit her father Mr Beaufort at Holly Rectory (132), they are joined in due course by the younger Grenvilles in the company of Mrs Melville and her own two children, who all stay until the winter sets in (133) before returning to Bellemere. In the meantime, Mr and Mrs Grenville take their eldest children, Eleanor and Augusta, on a picturesque tour to Northumbria and the Highlands and islands of Scotland, before they also make their way back to Bellemere. Several of the places they visited must have been well-known to the Yelloly family, since Dr Yelloly was born in Northumberland and they regularly toured in the north of the country (134-7). Improvements have been undertaken at Bellemere, perhaps in the family's absence: the breakfast room is shown 'new furnished', the chairs in scarlet case-covers, informally placed in the middle of the room, rather than set stiffly against the wall as hitherto was the custom, the walls painted a fashionable pink, the paintings re-hung, and a boldly patterned green carpet installed, similar to others in the album (142). In the schoolroom there is a handsome new upright piano (147), and Mrs Grenville is shown watering the flowers in what may be a new conservatory (143), by the 1820s an almost essential adjunct to any country house with pretensions to elegance.

The following spring, Mrs Grenville's brother, Sir Thomas Delville of Longwood Hall, his wife and two daughters, together with Sir Robert and Lady Harcourt of Merfleur Priory and their two daughters, who are also cousins of the Grenville children, all visit one another's houses, although the men are conspicuous by their absence from the *Picture History*. At the end of their visit, the Harcourts are accompanied home to Merfleur by the Grenville family, where Mary sets several scenes, including playtime in the nursery (145) and Augusta at work painting in watercolour (144), the only such depiction in the entire album, again a reflection of reality, for this might almost represent Mary Yelloly herself or one of her sisters at work on other *Picture Histories*.

Volume 4 ends with the appointment of Mr Weston's sister as the children's new governess, an appropriate and imaginative conclusion.

Whether or not further volumes of Mary Yelloly's *Picture History of the Grenville Family* were intended, this is the final one to have survived, all four being carefully bound into an album after her sadly early death in June 1838. In recording her surroundings and simple everyday activities with charm and directness, Mary Yelloly allows us to be transported into her own world and that of her imaginary family, the Grenvilles, to witness a uniquely engaging domestic drama that evokes a long-vanished and more innocent way of life.

T H E   F A M I L Y

MR   &   MRS   GRENVILLE
MISS   BEAUFORT   THE   GOVERNESS

A N D

T H E I R   C H I L D R E N

ELEANOR   *14 years*

AUGUSTA   *13 years*

MARIA   LOUISA   *9 years*

CHARLES   *7 years*

SOPHIA AGNES   *5 years*

HENRY THEODORE   *3 years*

OF

ROSEDALE   HOUSE,   WOODLANDS   HALL   &
BELLEMERE   PARK

Bellemere Park North View

View near Bellemere

Cottage at Bellemere

School Room Bellemere

Maria Louisa Sophia & Miss Beaufort

Mrs Fennington
who is come to spend six weeks there

Spare room Rectory

Mrs Melville & her baby

Dressing Room Bellemere
Mrs Fennington writing to annouce

Mrs Grenville's Sitting Room
bringing a flower of her own raising to her

Eleanor and Maria Louisa.
the Nurse bringing them the meat bought
with their own money for a poor sick woman

Colly Rectory where M.ʳ & M.ʳˢ Melville go with Maria Louisa to stop.

Mrs Smight's Cottage near
Holly-place. As the winter is come on.
Mrs Melville takes the little Grenvilles

Hermitage Castle

Roxburgh Sh

Ossians Hall and bridge
Perth Sh

Castle on Holy-Island

Naworth Castle Cumberland

Miss Beaufort's Room
used for the present as the Schoolroom
Eleanor Augusta & Maria Louisa making clothes

Housekeeper's Room

View near Bellemere.
Nurse, and Sophia Agnes.

View near Bellemere.
Nurse, and Sophia Agnes.

Breakfast Room Bellemere

new Furnished

Conservatory Bellemere
Mrs Grenville watering her flowers

Sitting Room Merfleur
Lady Harcourt Augusta & Sophia

Spare Room Merfleur P.

Now used as a Nursery for the little Grenvilles

Sitting Room Merfleur

School Room Bellemere

Mrs G's Sitting Room
Maria Louisa giving a poor woman

Rustic Arbour

Endnotes

[1] Florence Horatia Nelson Suckling, *A Forgotten Past*, London, 1898. This invaluable family memoir establishes that Mary Yelloly's album was part of a sequence. The author was the daughter of Admiral Suckling and married a cousin, Thomas Suckling, who was Mrs Yelloly's grandson, in 1876. Her name honoured their mutual ancestor, Admiral Horatio Nelson.

[2] Her date of birth is recorded on her memorial tablet in Woodton Church, Norfolk; she was baptised at St. Luke's, Old Street, London, 18 June 1818.

[3] Interestingly, Mary Ellen Best (1809-1891), whose watercolours made in the 1830s and 1840s recording daily life in Yorkshire and then in Germany, where she married and settled, came from a virtually identical background; her father, Dr Best (1779-1817), had studied at Edinburgh, and was briefly a physician at the Carey Street Dispensary, London, before returning to York, where he became physician to the city's Lunatic Asylum. Her mother came from a local landowning family. C. Davidson, *The World of Mary Ellen Best*, London, 1985.

[4] E. Bateson, *History of Northumberland*, vol. II, Kent, 1895, p.412.

[5] J. Curling, *Edward Wortley Montagu 1713-1776, The Man in the Iron Wig*, London, 1954, pp.168, 170; W. S. Lewis (ed.), *Horace Walpole's Correspondence*, vol. XXII, New Haven, 1960, pp.76-7, 113.

[6] Sarah Yelloly died 21 October 1854, leaving a very detailed will (PROB 11/2203).

[7] In the late 1890s, the Rev. C. W. Lohr recalled that 'the Yellolys were always very kind to the poor'. F. H. Suckling, *op. cit.*, p.113.

[8] Dr Yelloly's medical career is well summarised in P. Hunting, *The History of the Royal Society of Medicine*, London, 2002, pp.10-17, 36-7, 70.

[9] N. G. Coley, 'Alexander Marcet (1770-1822), Physician and Animal Chemist', *Medical History*, vol. XII, 1968, pp.394-402.

[10] The Norfolk connection is significant in the light of Yelloly's marriage and subsequent career. See G. Richardson, 'A Norfolk Network within the Royal Society', *Notes and Records of the Royal Society*, vol. 56 (1), 2002, pp.27-39.

[11] P. Hunting, *op. cit.*, p.17. Yelloly was responsible for finding the first premises for the Society and founding its library, became its first Honorary Secretary and in 1834 proposed and secured the Society's Royal Charter. His portrait by John Jackson belongs to the Society.

[12] F. H. Suckling, *op. cit.*, p.74.

Endnotes

[13] F. H. Suckling, *op. cit.*, pp.71-2.

[14] Samuel Tyssen died intestate 31 October 1800. As Administrator of his estate, Sir Joseph Banks arranged for the dispersal of his collections; there were no less than six auctions at Sotheby's between March 1802 and December 1803 (F. Lugt, *Répertoire des Catalogues de Ventes*, vol. I, The Hague, 1938, nos. 6381, 6404, 6435, 6522, 6553, 6726). Lady Banks (née Dorothy Hugesson) was Samuel Tyssen's second cousin. Sarah Tyssen's grandmother, Sarah Boddicott, died 11 November 1800.

[15] F. H. Suckling, *op. cit.*, pp.76-7.

[16] Anthony Vandyke Copley Fielding (1787-1855), one of the most fashionable and successful watercolourists of his day, was chiefly based in the northwest of England until 1809, when he moved to London. By this date, Mrs Yelloly had been married for three years; she had almost certainly received professional tuition as a girl, but of course it is possible that she took the occasional lesson from Copley Fielding, given her serious interest in watercolour painting.

[17] A. Bermingham, *Learning to Draw: Studies in the Cultural History of a Polite and Useful Art*, New Haven & London, 2000, is a comprehensive account both of the practice of amateur drawing as a polite accomplishment, and of the cultural context in which this took place, in particular the status of women.

[18] PROB 11/1963.

[19] Philip Meadows Martineau was one of the most distinguished lithotomists of his day. A. Batty Shaw, 'The Norwich School of Lithotomy', *Medical History*, vol. XIV, 1970, pp.243-8 *passim*.

[20] Yelloly had first published a paper on urinary calculi in *Transactions of the Medical & Chirurgical Society*, vol. VI, 1815, pp.574-82.

[21] F. H. Suckling, *op. cit.*, p.99.

[22] J. K. Crellin, 'Mrs Marcet's *Conversations on Chemistry*', *Journal of Chemical Education*, vol. LVI, 1979, pp.459-60. The Yellolys kept in close contact with Mrs Marcet and her children following her husband's death in 1822, visiting her when they were in London.

[23] S. Lasdun, *Victorians at Home*, London, 1981, pp.34-44.

[24] F. H. Suckling, *op. cit.*, pp.103-4, 106-9. None of Sarah's journals – or Mary's – appears to have survived.

[25] F. H. Suckling, *op. cit.*, p. 104.

[26] F. H. Suckling, *op. cit.*, pp.106, 110,119-21.

Endnotes

[27] The height at which Mary Yelloly shows pictures hanging may partly be childish distortion, but see C. Davidson, *op. cit.*, p.28. The carpets, in apparently improbably bright colours and bold designs that recur throughout Mary Yelloly's album, are almost certainly not imaginary, simplified though the patterns are. Mary Ellen Best painted several comparable examples, C. Davidson, *op. cit.*, pp.28, 36, 50. Humphry Repton showed a very similar carpet in his plate 'Window at Barningham Hall, Norfolk', in *Fragments on the Theory and Practice of Landscape Gardening*, 1816.

[28] A substantial literature on the history of interiors has developed in the past thirty years or so, but the late J. Cornforth's *English Interiors 1790-1848: The Quest for Comfort*, London, 1978, remains one of the best introductions and includes a substantial number of illustrations, many by amateurs. He would have been intrigued by Mary Yelloly's album. Many of the details she observes literally, but with childish naivety, may be recognised in more sophisticated works.

[29] M. R. Blacker, *Flora Domestica: A History of Flower Arranging 1500-1930*, London, 2000.

[30] A. Bermingham, *op. cit.*, discusses the influence of such manuals.

[31] She bequeathed this to her son John.

[32] Woodton Hall was demolished c.1840. A watercolour by H. N. Rolfe after an earlier view by the Rev. Alfred Suckling, c.1820, is illustrated in J. Kenworthy-Browne, *Burke's and Savills Guide to Country Houses*, vol. III (East Anglia), London, 1981, p.209.

[33] These appeared at Christie's 17 Nov. 1994, lot 11.

[34] F. H. Suckling, *op. cit.*, p.110.

[35] F. H. Suckling, *op. cit.*, pp.111-13.

[36] F. H. Suckling, *op. cit.*, pp. 114, 122.